BITCOIN

EXPLAINED

INTRODUCTION GUIDE TO THE CRYPTO CURRENCY AND BITCOIN WORLD

CONTAINS TWO BOOKS:

BITCOIN: WHAT IS BITCOIN?

BITCOIN: BTC AND BCH WHAT IS THE DIFFERENCE?

Table of Contents

Bitcoin: What is Bitcoin?

BITCOIN: BTC AND BCH

Bitcoin: What is Bitcoin?

Why should you start buying small amounts for the future?

Johan von Amsterdam

INTRODUCTION

I want to thank you and congratulate you for purchasing the book,

'Bitcoin: What is Bitcoin?'.

This book contains proven steps for how to setup your Bitcoin app on your mobile and how you can acquire and buy your first Bitcoins.

Bitcoin was introduced back in 2009. This book will cover the history, the advantages compared with the money controlled by governments and the possible downsides and risks you should take into account when you want to invest in it.

It gives you an introduction to the block chain technology and smart contracts principle.

The book will show you the different ways to store your Bitcoin keys and guides you in the first steps to acquire, buy and sell Bitcoins.

After reading this book you will be able to buy your own Bitcoins, make a decision where and how to store your

Bitcoins, and how to sell Bitcoins. You will get advice regarding your Bitcoin investment strategies.

Thanks again for purchasing this book, I hope you enjoy it!

fiat - an arbitrary order
or decree

fiat money - backed by the government
that issues it.
page 19

1 CRYPTOCURRENCY: THE FUTURE OF FINANCIAL TRANSACTIONS

If you are asked what the birth of cryptocurrency would bring to the world of finance, the first thing that will probably cross your mind is what is cryptocurrency? This thought however, will only come to the mind of people who are not well versed with the existing online currencies. But, if you are one of the few but dominant figures who know cryptocurrencies even if your eyes are closed, you would be able to answer the question more elaborately.

So to speak, the actual start of the turmoil existed when Bitcoin was introduced to the world and eventually became the most famous and wanted cryptocurrency. This project was started primarily to answer the lingering complaints of people whose money and assets are held by one centralized unit (and often intervened by the government itself) and whose transfers are limited and frozen at a timely basis. With the start of Bitcoin, many had the option to acquire an online coin or currency that they can use similarly with fiat money. Although acquiring it is tedious and requires resources, many were attracted to it from the very start because many were wanting to break away with the confinement of a single entity controlling everything else in terms of finance.

Slowly, Bitcoin started to gain actual monetary value and new types of cryptocurrencies came into existence as a possible answer to the problems that Bitcoin imposes and also to create their own currencies that people can opt to use as the one generated from the former is limited and hard to acquire.

Although cryptocurrency was not widely accepted, it slowly gained its momentum and now, many other businesses even accept it as a form of payment or exchange. The very same thing is slowly happening to new crypto currencies. Although the profits are not guaranteed and the software running them is open-source, many still try to vie to acquire these currencies as another means of investment.

If this kind of merge between technology and finance continues to improve over time, it will be no wonder if more and more people will divert their attention to acquiring these coins and more businesses will open themselves to exchanging and accepting them as actual reward or trade for goods and services. Like everything else, the slow but steady approach of crypto currency could result in major changes in the way finance has been seen and treated in the past.

More people are opening their minds to the existence and stability of such platforms and many are craving to break away from the scrutinizing eyes of the governing bodies involved in the storage and exchange of their assets. The future may seem dim this day but as more creative minds work together to make more convenience in the way finance and everything monetary is treated. Who knows maybe one day even fiat money can disappear for good.

The question that remains now would be if the government will allow such major changes that will incur their ~~lost~~ loss? or will such things also change the way our government runs and thinks.

2 INTRODUCTION TO BLOCKCHAIN

If you've attempted to dive into this mysterious thing called blockchain, you'd be forgiven for recoiling in horror at the sheer opaqueness of the technical jargon that is often used to frame it. So before we get into what a Bitcoin is we need to know how blockchain technology might change the world, let's discuss what blockchain actually is.

In the simplest terms, a blockchain is a digital ledger of transactions, not unlike the ledgers we have been using for hundreds of years to record sales and purchases. The function of this digital ledger is, in fact, pretty much identical to a traditional ledger in that it records debits and credits between people. That is the core concept behind blockchain; the difference is who holds the ledger and who verifies the transactions.

With traditional transactions, a payment from one person to another involves some kind of intermediary to facilitate the transaction. Let's say Rob wants to transfer $20 to Melanie. He can either give her cash in the form of a $20 note, or he can use some kind of banking app to transfer the money directly to her bank account. In both cases, a bank is the intermediary verifying the transaction: Rob's funds are verified when he takes the money out of a cash machine, or they are verified by the app when he makes the digital transfer. The bank decides if the transaction should go ahead. The bank also holds the record of all transactions made by Rob, and is solely responsible for updating it whenever Rob pays someone or receives money into his account. In other words, the bank holds and controls the ledger, and everything flows through the bank.

That's a lot of responsibility, so it's important that Rob feels he can trust his bank otherwise he would not risk his money with them. He needs to feel confident that the bank will not defraud him, will not lose his money, will not be robbed, and will not disappear overnight. This need for trust has underpinned pretty much every major behaviour and facet of the monolithic finance industry, to the extent that even when it was discovered that banks were being irresponsible with our money during the financial crisis of 2008, the government (another intermediary) chose to bail them out rather than risk destroying the final fragments of trust by letting them collapse.

Blockchains operate differently in one key respect: they are entirely decentralised. There is no central clearing house like a bank, and there is no central ledger held by one entity. Instead, the ledger is distributed across a vast network of

7

computers, called nodes, each of which holds a copy of the entire ledger on their respective hard drives. These nodes are connected to one another via a piece of software called a peer-to-peer (P2P) client, which synchronises data across the network of nodes and makes sure that everybody has the same version of the ledger at any given point in time.

When a new transaction is entered into a blockchain, it is first encrypted using state-of-the-art cryptographic technology. Once encrypted, the transaction is converted to something called a block, which is basically the term used for an encrypted group of new transactions. That block is then sent (or broadcast) into the network of computer nodes, where it is verified by the nodes and, once verified, passed on through the network so that the block can be added to the end of the ledger on everybody's computer, under the list of all previous blocks. This is called the chain, hence the tech is referred to as a blockchain.

Once approved and recorded into the ledger, the transaction can be completed. This is how cryptocurrencies like Bitcoin work.

what is a computer node?

Accountability and the removal of trust

What are the advantages of this system over a banking or central clearing system? Why would Rob use Bitcoin instead of normal currency?

The answer is trust. As mentioned before, with the banking system it is critical that Rob trusts his bank to protect his money and handle it properly. To ensure this happens, enormous regulatory systems exist to verify the actions of the banks and ensure they are fit for purpose. Governments then regulate the regulators, creating a sort of tiered system of checks whose sole purpose is to help prevent mistakes and bad behaviour. In other words, organisations like the Financial Services Authority exist precisely because banks can't be trusted on their own. And banks frequently make mistakes and misbehave, as we have seen too many times. When you have a single source of authority, power tends to get abused or misused. The trust relationship between people and banks is awkward and precarious: we don't really trust them but we don't feel there is much alternative.

Blockchain systems, on the other hand, don't need you to trust them at all. All transactions (or blocks) in a blockchain are verified by the nodes in the network before being added to the ledger, which means there is no single point of failure and no single approval channel. If a hacker wanted to successfully tamper with the ledger on a blockchain, they would have to simultaneously hack millions of computers, which is almost impossible. A hacker would also be pretty much unable to bring a blockchain network down, as, again, they would need to be able to shut down every single computer in a network of computers distributed around the world.

The encryption process itself is also a key factor. Blockchains like the Bitcoin one use deliberately difficult processes for their verification procedure. In the case of Bitcoin, blocks are verified by nodes performing a deliberately processor- and time-intensive series of calculations, often in the form of puzzles or complex mathematical problems, which mean that verification is neither instant nor accessible. Nodes that do commit the resource to verification of blocks are rewarded with a transaction fee and a bounty of newly-minted Bitcoins. This has the function of both incentivising people to become nodes (because processing blocks like this requires pretty powerful computers and a lot of electricity), whilst also handling the process of generating - or minting - units of the currency. This is referred to as mining, because it involves a considerable amount of effort (by a computer, in this case) to produce a new commodity. It also means that transactions are verified by the most independent way possible, more independent than a government-regulated organisation like the FSA.

This decentralised, democratic and highly secure nature of blockchains means that they can function without the need for regulation (they are self-regulating), government or other opaque intermediary.

Let the significance of that sink in for a while and the excitement around blockchain starts to make sense.

Smart contracts

Where things get really interesting is the applications of blockchain beyond cryptocurrencies like Bitcoin. Given that one of the underlying principles of the blockchain system is the secure, independent verification of a transaction, it's easy to imagine other ways in which this type of process can be valuable. Unsurprisingly, many such applications are already in use or development.

Some of the best ones are:

Smart contracts (Ethereum): probably the most exciting blockchain development after Bitcoin, smart contracts are blocks that contain code that must be executed in order for the contract to be fulfilled. The code can be anything, as long as a computer can execute it, but in simple terms it means that you can use blockchain technology (with its independent verification, trustless architecture and security) to create a kind of escrow system for any kind of transaction. As an example, if you're a web designer you could create a contract that verifies if a new client's website is launched or not, and then automatically release the funds to you once it is. No more chasing or invoicing. Smart contracts are also being used to prove ownership of an asset such as property or art. The potential for reducing fraud with this approach is enormous.

Cloud storage: cloud computing has revolutionised the web and brought about the advent of Big Data which has, in turn, kick started the new AI revolution. But most cloud-based systems are run on servers stored in single-location server farms, owned by a single entity (Amazon, Rackspace, Google etc). This presents all the same problems as the banking system, in that your data is controlled by a single, opaque organisation which represents a single point of failure. Distributing data on a blockchain removes the trust issue entirely and also promises to increase reliability as it is so much harder to take a blockchain network down.

Digital identification: two of the biggest issues of our time are identify theft and data protection. With vast centralised services such as Facebook holding so much data about us, and efforts by various developed-world governments to store digital information about their citizens in a central database, the potential for abuse of our personal data is terrifying. Blockchain technology offers a potential solution to this by wrapping your key data up into an encrypted block that can be verified by the blockchain network whenever you need to prove your identity. The applications of this range from the obvious replacement of passports and I.D. cards to other areas such as replacing passwords. It could be huge.

Digital voting: highly topical in the wake of the investigation into Russia's influence on the recent U.S. election, digital voting has long been suspected of being both unreliable and highly vulnerable to tampering. Blockchain technology offers a way of verifying that a voter's vote was successfully sent while retaining their anonymity. It promises not only to reduce fraud in elections but also to increase general voter turnout as people will be able to vote on their mobile phones.

Blockchain technology is still very much in its infancy and most of the applications are a long way from general use. Even Bitcoin, the most established blockchain platform, is ?

subject to huge volatility indicative of its relative newcomer status. However, the potential for blockchain to solve some of the major problems we face today makes it an extraordinarily

form of blockchain?

13

exciting and seductive technology to follow. I will certainly be keeping an eye out.

3 WHY BITCOIN?

Bitcoin is known as the very first decentralized digital currency, they're basically coins that can ~~send~~ be sent through the Internet. 2009 was the year when bitcoin was born. The creator's name is unknown, however the alias Satoshi Nakamoto was given to this person.

Bitcoin transactions are made directly from person to person through the internet. There's no need of a bank or clearinghouse to act as the middle man. Thanks to that, the transaction fees are ~~way too~~ much lower, and they can be used in all the countries around the world. Bitcoin accounts cannot be frozen, prerequisites to open them don't exist, same for limits. Every day more merchants are starting to accept them. You can buy anything you want with them.

It's possible to exchange dollars, euros or other currencies to bitcoin. You can buy and sell as it were any other country's currency. In order to keep your bitcoins, you have to store them in something called wallets. These wallets are located in your pc, mobile device, on paper or in third party websites. Sending bitcoins is very simple. It's as simple as sending an email. You can purchase practically anything with bitcoins.

Bitcoin is a big deal right now, but not everyone understands why. More importantly, not everyone understands whether or not Bitcoin is for them, and how they can get involved. Here are some of the most compelling reasons why you should use Bitcoin.

More secure than banks

procedure for solving a problem
→ rule or procedure

The Bitcoin algorithm is as close to bulletproof as a computer program can get. Some of the best hackers and online security experts have taken a crack at it, and so far no one can find any weaknesses. The Bitcoin code has been described as masterfully written, the digital equivalent to Shakespeare.

Bank transactions, meanwhile, are under a lower level of security than Bitcoin. In many ways, Bitcoin is more secure than keeping money in the banks. That makes Bitcoin a target for those who would like to see it fail. But Bitcoin's inventor Satoshi Nakamoto kept this in mind while writing the Bitcoin algorithm. Go ahead, give it a shot. I don't think you'll be able to crack it.

Lower service fees than banks

Banking institutions charge high rates per transaction. The system is set up in a way that individual transactions between two people are impossible; they require a "trusted" third party to facilitate the transaction. And, naturally, the banks get to take a service fee for facilitating these transactions.

You can use escrow services with Bitcoin which take a service fee, but you don't have to. Because Bitcoin is based on P2P transactions, there are no service fees. Naturally, the banks aren't a big fan of Bitcoin because of this.

Low risk of inflation

Bitcoin volatility refers to how much the Bitcoin price jumps up and down over time.

This is a mathematical measure of the potential size of likely price changes. Relative volatility expectations explain why a 2% daily change in the value of a major currency may shock markets whereas a 4% daily move in Bitcoin is considered fairly standard.

Although the current Bitcoin volatility on the trading markets is very high, in the long run the risk of inflation is small. The number of Bitcoins being created is set at a predetermined rate. What that means is there is no possibility of any government printing off more money to pay off their debts. When the usage of this crypto currency becomes more common, the demand will rise and so will the price.

Whereas real world currencies lose a small percent of their worth every year. When your currency is attached to a government, it depends on the stability of that government. You and I both know governments can fall, and when they do the currency they printed can sometimes become worthless. Take a look at the bills in your wallet. You worked hard for them. Can you imagine them one day becoming worth less than the paper they were printed on?

Bitcoin isn't perfect. Just like anything, there are risks involved. In the face of increasing uncertainty in the global market, Bitcoin seems to be quickly becoming a beacon of stability and an exciting opportunity to create a new financial world.

4 OTHER CHARACTERISTICS OF BITCOIN

Bitcoin has the characteristics of traditional currencies such as purchasing power, and investment applications using online trading instruments. It works just like conventional money, only in the sense that it can only exist in the digital world.

One of its unique attributes that cannot be matched by Fiat currency (Fiat currency is legal tender whose value is backed by the government that issued it. The U.S. dollar is fiat money, as are the euro and many other major world currencies) is that it is decentralized. The currency does not run under a governing body or an institution, which means it cannot be controlled by these entities, giving users full ownership of their bitcoins.

Bitcoin Anonymity

When doing a Bitcoin transaction, there's no need to provide the real name of the person. Each one of the bitcoin transactions are recorded is what is known as a public log. This log contains only wallet IDs and not people's names, so basically each transaction is private. People can buy and sell things without being tracked.

Moreover, transactions occur with the use of Bitcoin addresses, which are not linked to any names, addresses, or any personal information asked for by traditional payment systems.

Every single Bitcoin transaction is stored in a ledger anyone can access, this is called the blockchain. If a user has a publicly used address, its information is shared for everyone to see, without its user's information of course.

Bitcoin innovation

Accounts are easy to create, unlike conventional banks that requests for countless information, which may put its users in jeopardy due to the frauds and schemes surrounding the system.

Furthermore, Bitcoin transactions fees will always be small in number. Apart from near-instant completion of processing, no fees are known to be significant enough to put a dent on one's account.

Bitcoin established a whole new way of innovation. The Bitcoin software is all open source, this means anyone can review it. A nowadays fact is that bitcoin is transforming world's finances similar to how web changed everything about publishing. The concept is brilliant. When everyone has access to the whole Bitcoin global market, new ideas appear. Transaction fees reductions is a fact of bitcoin. Accepting Bitcoins cost anything, also they're very easy to setup. Charge backs don't exist. The Bitcoin community will generate additional businesses of all kinds.

5 WHAT IS A BITCOIN WALLET?

A Bitcoin wallet is a piece of software that contains the "keys" and the address that allows you to send and receive bitcoins.

In the same way that Paypal uses an email address, the bitcoin protocol uses an address like 1JArS6jzE3AJ9sZ3aFij1BmTcpFGgN86hA extracted from the public keys stored in your wallet.

Most bitcoins are stored in what is called digital wallets. These wallets exist in the cloud or in people's computers. A wallet is something similar to a virtual bank account. These wallets allow persons to send or receive Bitcoins, pay for things or just save the Bitcoins. Opposed to bank accounts, these bitcoin wallets are never insured by the Federal Deposit Insurance Corporation (FDIC). The FDIC insures the deposits of bank customers against bank failure. The insurance premium is paid by nationally licensed banks to FDIC and they pay out benefits in the event of a bank going down.

The FDIC's mission is to protect depositors in the event of a bank failure, and maintain citizens' confidence in the banking system. When a bank fails, FDIC steps in and first attempts to get another bank to take over, for example when JP Morgan took over Washington Mutual.

In this book we'll show you the main types of wallets and how to create one, step by step with blockchain.info.

Have you ever wondered how to step in into the bitcoin world?

You are in the right place.

Types of Bitcoin Wallet

A Bitcoin wallet is like to your bank account. It is used to store, send and receive Bitcoins. A Bitcoin wallet stores the private keys and public keys. The public key is used to send/receive money and the private key is what actually gives you access to your account. Below are different types of Bitcoin wallet you can use.

1. Web or Wallet in the cloud

The most used and the easiest to set up.

It's accesible through your web browser and it's stored in the servers of the service provider.

It works in the same way as typical email clients, like Gmail or Yahoo.

Wallet in cloud: the advantage of having a wallet in the cloud is that people don't need to install any software in their computers and wait for long syncing processes. The disadvantage is that <u>the cloud may be hacked and people may lose their bitcoins</u>. Nevertheless, these sites are very secure. Be very careful with ~~like~~ drag and drop ~~of~~ documents into the cloud storage folder. This could permanently move the document. Instead do copy and paste, and Also Accessibility; If you have no internet connection, you have no access to your data.

2. Desktop Wallets
Bitcoin

They are installed on your computer and allow you to fully control the wallet because <u>private keys</u> are stored locally.

What is this?

There are two types:

Full Clients, which download the entire blockchain and Lightweight Clients, that store the private keys locally but they don't download the entire blockchain, accessing ~~to~~ it instead through proxy servers.

The advantage of having a wallet on the computer is that people keep their Bitcoins secured from the rest of the internet. The disadvantage is that people may delete them by formatting the computer or because of viruses.

3. Mobile

↙ ? Bitcoin Wallet

They can work as Full Clients, Lightweight Clients or Web Clients.

Wallets

Some ~~of them~~ are <u>cross-platform</u>, linked with web or desktop clients, sharing the same source of bitcoins. *? ? ?*

4. Hardware

As pendrives, paper wallets or some other device types.

↑ ?

6 HOW TO CREATE A BITCOIN WALLET

The easiest and fastest way to get started in the bitcoin world is by creating a web wallet.

There are several well proven providers *such* as Coinbase or Blockchain. Both provide web wallets, an android app and an iPhone app.

In this guide we will use the blockchain web wallet due to its ease of use, simplicity and popularity.

Creating the Wallet

Go to blockchain.info and press "Create Wallet".

You will be asked for an email address that will be used to verify your identity each time you try to open your wallet (optional) and a password.

It's important to use a password as strong as you can think of with more than 10 characters, low and uppercase letters, numbers and symbols.

When finished, you will be asked to write and store a phrase that will be used to get access to your wallet if you forget your password.

This is important because there is no way to recover it if you lose your password.

Accessing the wallet

Once created and verified through the confirmation email, you are set to open it and start operating with Bitcoins.
Is the wallet

To do it you have to introduce the identifier included in the mail and the password.
logged on? inside the wallet? Once the wallet is open

Once inside you will see the control panel of your wallet from which you can access your transaction history, the options for sending and receiving Bitcoins, the account settings and several options for backing up your wallet, something terribly important .

Receiving money

The first thing to do to receive bitcoins in your wallet is to
what
know ~~which~~ your address is.

You can see it in the control panel of your wallet as a QR or as an alphanumeric code. *(letters + numbers)*

Share it so people can send you money through it.

Sending money

To send bitcoins you must click on the option and indicate the direction to which you want to send them and the amount.

Buying Bitcoins from the market

To directly exchange your dollars or euros ~~are~~ ^{or} other fiat currency you can choose the option buy Bitcoins. You will get the current rate and the transaction cost and if you proceed you can setup a your SEPA bank account for European banks. This ~~to~~ avoids additional transactions costs. Both Visa and Mastercards are accepted. This is one of the most commonly used options if you want to invest in Bitcoins. At the moment the maximum amount per transaction is U$ 250,-. (2017)

$250K

Transaction History

You can view the transaction history and its details by clicking on "My Transactions".

Here you will see the pair of adresses, the date on which the operation was performed, the amount sent/received and the number of confirmations.

That's it.

You already have the main tool that lets you step into the Bitcoin world.

About commissions, confirmations and thieves

Although compared to the traditional banking system operations bitcoins are much cheaper, faster and safer, that does not make them free, instant or impossible to intercept.

Commissions

When sending Bitcoins you will see that the amount received is slightly smaller than the amount sent.

These fees are the incentive for miners to provide computing power to the Bitcoin network and keep the system running.

You can adjust the commission when making shipping but keep in mind that if it's very low, the transaction will take longer to be confirmed.

Confirmations

To avoid fraud, transactions in the bitcoin protocol must be confirmed by the network.

The system is designed so that each block of transactions is mined in about 10 minutes.

Security

Both the Bitcoin protocol and the majority of wallets are equipped with security layers that prevent your money is accessible to "foreign friends" with ease.

However, no system is perfect.

Other ways to store your Bitcoins

You don't usually carry 3.000 $ in your pocket, right? Due to the same reasons you don't do this, the same applies to bitcoin.

You shouldn't store all your Bitcoins in the same place. Luckily, there are several ways to do this and most of them are free or at a low cost.

Two of the most common are:

Cold Storage: Cold storage refers to keep your Bitcoins offline. This can be done in different ways (link to knowledge base), as in servers disconnected from the network, USB flash drives or paper wallets.

30

Creating other wallets: You can create as many wallets as you want and store in them the bitcoins you have. A common practice is to deposit a certain amount in the wallet more used to operate and leave the bulk of your bitcoins in another.

7 GETTING YOUR
FIRST FREE BITCOINS

Now that you have a wallet, you will, of course, want to test them out.

The very first place to go is http://faucet.Bitcoin.st.

This is a website that gives out small amounts of bitcoin for the purpose of getting people used to using them. The original version of this was run by the lead developer of bitcoin, Gavin Andreson. That site has since closed and this site operates by sending out one or two advertisements a month. You agree to receive those messages by requesting the Bitcoins. Copy and paste your new bitcoin address and enter a phone number to which you can receive an SMS. They send out an SMS to be

faucet . Bitcoin . st

sure that people are not continuously coming back for more since it costs nothing to create a bitcoin address. They will also send out once or twice a month *an* advertisement to support their operation. The amount they send is trivial: 0.0015 BTC (or 1.5 mBTC). However, they process almost immediately and you can check to see that your address and wallet are working. It is also quite a feeling to get that portion of a bitcoin. (Non-disclaimer: I have no connection with this site

SMS ?

32

and receive nothing if you use them. I simply think they are a good way to get your feet wet).

Congratulations! You have just entered the bitcoin economy.

To get your feet a little wetter, you can go panning for gold. There are a number of services and websites out there that will pay you in bitcoin to do things like go to certain websites, fill out online surveys, or watch sponsored videos. These are harmless, and you can earn a few extra bitcoins this way, but it is important to remember that these are businesses that get paid when people click on the links on their sites. They are essentially kicking back a portion of what they get paid to you. There is nothing illegal, or even immoral about this (you might like what you see and make a purchase!), but they are frequently flashy and may not be completely straightforward. All the ones that I have tried (particularly bitvisitor.com) have paid out as advertised. It is interesting to experiment with these, but even with the likely rise in the value of Bitcoin, you won't become a millionaire doing this. So, unless you are an advertisement junkie, I would recommend you move on. If you would like to try, simply Google "free bitcoins" or something along those lines and you will find numerous sites.

8 BUYING BITCOIN
HAND-TO-HAND

Finally, this is going to be the real test of Bitcoin. Can people easily trade them back and forth? If this can't happen, then there can't really be a bitcoin economy because retailers won't be able to use it. If retailers can't use it, what earthly good is it? Fortunately, this is not really a problem. iPhone is a bit of a hold out, but many smartphones have apps (mobile wallets) that will read QR codes and allow you to send bitcoin to whomever you want. You can also display a QR code of your address, or even carry a card in your wallet with your QR code to let people send Bitcoin to you. Depending on what kind of wallet you have, you can then check to see if the Bitcoins have been received.

A couple of things to note:

When you set up your wallet, if you click around a bit, you will see an option to pay a fee to speed transactions. This money becomes available to a bitcoin miner as he/she/they process Bitcoin information. The miners doing the work of creating blocks of information keeps the system up to date and secure. The fee is an incentive to the miner to be sure to include your information in the next information block and therefore "verify" it. In the short term, miners are making most of their money by mining new coins (check the section on What Are Bitcoins for more information about this). In the long term, as it gets harder to find new coins, and as the economy increases, the fees will be an incentive for miners to keep creating more blocks and keep the economy going. Your wallet should be set to pay 0 fees as a default, but if you want, you can add a fee to prioritize your transactions. You are under no obligation to pay a fee, and many organizations that process many small transactions (like the ones that pan for gold described above) produce enough fees to keep the miners happy.

In clicking around your wallet, on the transactions page or linked to specific transactions, you will see a note about confirmations. When you make a transaction, that information is sent out into the network and the network will send back a confirmation that there is no double entry for that Bitcoin. It is smart to wait until you get several confirmations before walking away from someone who has paid you. It is actually not very easy to scam someone hand-to-hand like this, and it is not very cost-effective for the criminal, but it can be done.

Where can you buy bitcoin like this?

Blockchain and Coinbase

Bitcoin is the pinnacle of mobile money. The Bitcoin apps are becoming increasingly popular. Programmers are moving into the market to meet the growing demand of making it easier to buy and sell Bitcoin.

Smartphones are our constant companions, and there are many Bitcoin wallet apps on the Google Play Store, but the issue is finding one that fits your particular needs.

The Wallet you set up in chapter 6 on Blockchain is also accessible through downloadable Google Play Store and the iPhone App Store apps.

The other platform mentioned before, Coinbase, was founded in 2012. It also has apps for both iOS and Android, and it has inbuilt wallets for bitcoins, ether, litecoins and the good old US dollar. The wallet require a three-step verification process in order to access the Coinbase app. The Coinbase app also shows nice graphs about the market value of the crypto currencies, the last hour, the last 24 hours, the last week, the last month and the last year.

Coinbase ?

It requires an extensive identity verification process during signup, documents such as Proof of ID and residency have to be sent over and reviewed, similar to opening a bank account.

The app is incredibly user friendly, and can instantly convert Bitcoins, ethereum and litecoins to dollars and other fiat currencies and vice versa by using its built-in wallets for both currencies.

We have other mobile apps like:

- Copay

- Mycelium

- Bitpay

- Gliph

- Spare

- Fold and so on.

You may have a bitcoin Meetup in your area.

You can check out localbitcoins.com to find people near you who are interested in buying or selling.

Some are trying to start up local street exchanges across the world. These are called Buttonwoods after the first street exchange established on Wall Street in 1792 under a buttonwood tree. See if there is one, or start one, in your area.

See if you have any friends who would like to try bitcoins out. Actually, the more people who start using bitcoin, the larger and more successful it will be come. So please tell two friends!

Some people ask if it is possible to buy physical bitcoins. The answer to this is both a yes and a no. Bitcoin, by its very nature, is a digital currency and has no physical form. However, there are a couple of ways that you can practically hold a bitcoin in your hands:

Cascascius Coins: These are the brainchild of Mike Caldwell. He mints physical coins and then embeds the private keys for the bitcoins inside them. You can get the private key by peeling a hologram from the coin which will then clearly show that the coin has been tampered with. Mike has gone out of his way to ensure that he can be trusted. These are a good investment strategy as in the years to come it may be that these coins are huge collector's items.

Paper Wallets: A paper wallet just means that rather than keeping the information for your bitcoin stored in a digital wallet, you print the key information off along with a private key and keep it safe in a safe, in a drawer, or in your mattress (if you like). This is highly recommended and cost effective system for keeping your Bitcoin safe. Keep in mind, though, that someone could steal them or if your house burns, they will go with the house and there will be no way to get them back. Really, no different than cash. Also, as with Casascius Coins, they will not really be good for spending until you put them back into the computer.

* There is software to make printing your paper wallets easier. bitcoinpaperwallet.com is one of the best and includes a good tutorial about how to use them.

* The bitcoins are not actually in the wallet, they are still on the web. In fact, the outside of the wallet will have a QR code that will allow you to ship coins to the wallet any time you like.

* The sealed part of the wallet will have the private key without which you cannot access the coins. Therefore, only put as many coins on the wallet as you want to be inaccessible. You will not be able to whip this thing out and take out a few coins to buy a cup of coffee. Rather, think of it as a piggy bank. To get the money, you have to smash it. It is possible to take out smaller amounts, but at this point the security of the wallet is compromised and it would be easier for someone to steal the coins. Better to have them all in or out.

* People who use paper wallets are usually security conscious, and there are a number of ways for the nefarious in the world

to hack your computer. Bitcoinpaperwallet.com gives a lot of good advice about how to print your wallets securely.

Some people have also asked about buying Bitcoins on eBay. Yes, it is possible, but they will be far overpriced. So, selling on eBay might seem to be a better option given the extreme markup over market value you might see. But, as with anything that is too good to be true, this is too good to be true. Selling bitcoin this way is just way too risky.

9 BITCOIN INVESTMENT STRATEGY

Apart from its abilities to purchase goods and services, one of its known applications features its use for a number of investment vehicles. This includes Forex (is a decentralized global market where all the world's currencies trade) trading Bitcoins, and binary options platforms. Furthermore, brands offer services that revolve around Bitcoin as currency.

Clearly, Bitcoin is as flexible as traditional legal tenders. Its introduction provides every individual with new beneficial opportunities with its ease of use and profit making capabilities. While the initial introduction of the technology came with a desktop program, it can now be directly operated through a smartphone application, which allows you to immediately buy, sell, trade or even cash your bitcoins for dollars.

This digital rush of money that is sweeping the global investors is not only getting easier, but also riskier everyday. While it was initially a simple peer-to-peer system for small transactions, it is now used for major investments and foreign luxury purchases, which has introduced newer strategies and uses. How does it really work?

The value

It is common knowledge it is improving the way transactions are being settled. The Bitcoin value relies heavily on how well the transaction fees are minimized; way below the transaction costs prevailing in the market. A professional broker understands better the value, which can help a great deal in ensuring sustained profits. The positive feedback being submitted daily on the benefits of brokers is creating a lot of enthusiasm. Many companies are relying on brokers because of the vast potential present within the arena of crypto currency. The system offers a quick and efficient way of executing financial transactions

Investment with Bitcoins has become very popular, with major sums of money being put in every day. As a new investor, the rules remain the same as investing with real cash. Do not invest more than you can afford to lose, and do not invest without a goal. For every trade, keep certain milestones in mind. The 'buy low and sell high' strategy is not as easy implemented as said. A great way to succeed faster when you decide to trade bitcoins, however, is to learn the technicalities. Like cash investments, there are now several bitcoin charting tools to record the marketing trends and make predictions to help you make investment decisions. Even as a beginner, learning how to use charting tools and how to read charts can go a long way. A normal chart will usually include the opening price, the closing price, the highest price, the lowest price and the trading range, which are the essentials you need before making any sale or purchase. Other components will give you different information about the market. For example, the 'order book' contains lists of prices and quantities that bitcoin traders are willing to buy and sell.

Moreover, new investors will often quickly open unprofitable positions. With this, however, remember that you have to pay an interest rate for every 24 hours that the position is kept open, with the exception of the first 24 hours that are free. Therefore, unless you have sufficient balance to cover the high interest rate, do not keep any unprofitable position open for more than 24 hours.

While Bitcoin trading still has its drawbacks, like transactions taking too long to complete and no reversing option, it can benefit you greatly with investing, provided that you take small steps in the right direction.

10 BITCOIN VOLATILITY

Traders are always concerned about 'Bitcoin''s volatility. It is important to know what makes the value of this particular digital currency highly unstable. Just like many other things, the value of 'Bitcoin' also depends upon the rules of demand and supply. If the demand for 'Bitcoin' increases, then the price will also increase. On the contrary side, the decrease in demand for the 'Bitcoin' will lead to decreased ~~demand~~ price. In simple words, we can say that the price is determined by what amount the trading market has agreed to pay. If a large number of people wish to purchase 'Bitcoin's, then the price will rise. If more folks want to sell 'Bitcoin's, then the price will come down.

It is worth knowing that the value of 'Bitcoin' can be volatile if compared to more established commodities and currencies. This fact can be credited to its comparatively small market size, which means that a lesser amount of money can shift the price of 'Bitcoin' more prominently. This inconsistency will reduce naturally over the passage of time as the currency develops and the market size grows.

After being teased in late 2016, 'Bitcoin' touched a new record high level in the first week of the current year. There could be several factors causing the 'Bitcoin' to be volatile. Some of these are discussed here.

The Bad Press Factor

'Bitcoin' users are mostly scared by different news events including the statements by government officials and geopolitical events that 'Bitcoin' can be possibly regulated. It means the rate of 'Bitcoin' adoption is troubled by negative or bad press reports. Different bad news stories created fear in investors and prohibited them from investing in this digital currency. An example of bad headline news is the eminent utilization of 'Bitcoin' in processing drug transactions through Silk Road which came to an end with the FBI stoppage of the market in October 2013. This sort of stories produced panic among people and caused the 'Bitcoin' value to decrease greatly. On the other side, veterans in the trading industry saw such negative incidents as an evidence that the 'Bitcoin' industry is maturing. So the 'Bitcoin' started to gain its increased value soon after the effect of bad press vanished.

Fluctuations of the Perceived Value

Another great reason for 'Bitcoin' value to become volatile is the fluctuation of the 'Bitcoin''s perceived value. You may know that this digital currency has properties akin to gold. This is ruled by a design decision by the makers of the core technology to restrict its production to a static amount, 21 million BTC. Due to this factor, investors may allocate less or more assets in into 'Bitcoin'.

News about Security Breaches

Various news agencies and digital media play an important role in building a negative or positive public concept. If you see something being advertised Advantageously, you are likely to go for that without paying much attention to negative sides. There has been news about 'Bitcoin' security breaches and it really made the investors think twice before investing their hard earned money in 'Bitcoin' trading. They become too susceptible about choosing any specific 'Bitcoin' investment platform. 'Bitcoin' may become volatile when 'Bitcoin' community uncovers security susceptibilities in an effort to create a great open source response in form of security fixes. Such security concerns give birth to several open-source software such as Linux. Therefore, it is advisable that 'Bitcoin' developers should expose security vulnerabilities to the general public in order to make strong solutions.

The latest 'OpenSSL' weaknesses attacked by 'Heartbleed' bug and reported by Neel Mehta (a member of Google's security team) on April 1, 2014, appear to had some descending effect on the value of 'Bitcoin'. According to some reports, the 'Bitcoin' value decreased up to 10% in the ensuing month as compared to the U.S. Dollar.

Small option value for holders of large 'Bitcoin' Proportions

The volatility of 'Bitcoin' also depends upon 'Bitcoin' holders having large proportions of this digital currency. It is not clear for 'Bitcoin' investors (with current holdings over $10M) that how they would settle a position that expands into a fiat position without moving the market severely. So 'Bitcoin' has not touched the bulk market adoption rates that would be important to give option value to large 'Bitcoin' holders.

Effects of Mt Gox

The recent high-profile damages at 'Mt Gox' are another great reason for the 'Bitcoin' volatility. All these losses and the resultant news about heavy losses had a dual effect on instability. You may not know that this reduced the general float of 'Bitcoin' by almost 5%. This also created a potential lift on the residual 'Bitcoin' value due to the reason of increased scarcity. Nevertheless, superseding this lift was the negative outcome of the news series that followed. Particularly, many other 'Bitcoin' gateways saw the large failure at Mt Gox as an optimistic thing for the long-term prospects of the 'Bitcoin'.

11 TIPS FOR NEW
BITCOIN TRADERS

Investors from around the globe are trying to cash in on the volatile Forex market, by trading with the crypto-currency, Bitcoin. Well, it is quite easy to get started with onlinetrading, but it is important for you to know that there are risks involved that you cannot afford to overlook.

As with any of the speculative or exchange markets, Bitcoin trading is also a dicey venture, which can possibly cost you a lot of money, especially if you don't get it right. Therefore, it is essential for you to know about the risks involved, before deciding to get started with it.

If you are a newbie, who is interested in trading with Bitcoin, then you will need to first understand the basics of trade and investing.

Avoid the common errors that new traders generally tend to make

Invest wisely

Any kind of financial investment can bring losses, instead of profits. Similarly, with the highly unstable Bitcoin market, you can expect both, profits and losses. It is all about making the right decisions at the right time.

Most of the beginners tend to lose money by making the wrong decisions that are generally driven by greed and poor analytical skills. Experts say that you should not venture into trading, if you are not ready to lose money. Basically, such an approach helps you in coping up mentally for the worst possibilities.

Diversify the portfolio

First, successful traders diversify their portfolios. Risk exposure increases if most of your funds are allocated for a single asset. It becomes harder for you to cover the losses from other assets. You cannot afford to lose more money than you invested, so avoid placing more funds on limited assets. It will help you sustain the negative trades to quite an extent.

Secondly, putting in more cash than you can afford, will also cloud your sound decision making abilities. In most cases, you will be compelled to opt for 'desperate selling' when market declines a little. Rather than holding through the market dip, the investor who has over-invested on the trade, is bound to panic. The person will feel the urge sell off the holding for a low price, in an attempt to lessen the losses.

You will also be losing more cash, when market recovers. It is because you will have to buy the same holding back, but at a higher price.

sounds like playing the stock market, "trading"

Set goals - Emotions make you blind

Goal setting for each transaction is vital when you trade Bitcoin. It helps you stay level-headed even in the extremely volatile conditions. Therefore, you will need to first determine the price to stop your losses.

The same rule also applies for profits, especially if you let your greed take over. The benefit of setting goals is that you can easily prevent making the decisions based on emotions.

Instead, you should work towards improving your skills for reading the charts and conducting the market analysis. It is also advisable for new traders to close their losing positions in 24 hours, so as to avoid paying the recurring interest.

If Bitcoin gets a adopted by big companies and a wider audience *tries to* will try the acquire them, then prices will rise even more. Personally, I am in for the long run and will wait a couple of years. I have set a date and / or price for which I will sell a part of my crypto currencies. What ever comes first. In the meanwhile I try to keep my emotions under control.

Why should you start buying small amounts for the future?

As mentioned there will be only a fixed amount of Bitcoins available. Bitcoin is around for many years already and more and more companies and countries accept it as a method for payments. The demand keeps rising and the exchange rates also. If you buy them now and keep them, before Bitcoin goes mainstrain, you can still make big profits is my personal view.

But of course this is a personal decision and nobody knows for sure what will happen with the future supply and demand of these currencies, hence what will happen with the price. So I strongly suggest that if you want to invest to only invest money you can actually miss if things don't turn out as expected.

CONCLUSION

Bitcoin is a decentralized peer to peer crypto-currency, and the first of its kind. It is one of the most fascinating innovations in finance in at least the last hundred years. Bitcoin is completely determined by an algorithm and everything is open-source so there are no surprises. No central agency can control the supply of Bitcoin, unlike fiat currencies or even materials like gold. The world can only ever see a total of 21 million Bitcoins in existence.

How do we know this?

Like any new disruptive innovation, Bitcoin has a fiercely loyal core group of supporters and followers who are passionate about the idea. They are the ones who take it forward and spread the idea and take it to the next level. Bitcoin has plenty of enthusiasts who are excited about the idea and how it can shape the future of finance, giving the power of money back to the masses instead of under a central control.

It is not just a passing fad. Bitcoin is here to stay. Miners are gearing up for the best of the best equipment to mine Bitcoin more effectively. Exchanges are investing heavily in the security and efficiency of the Bitcoin system. Entrepreneurs are taking their chances and building great businesses around this idea. Venture capital funds are beginning to support projects that revolve around Bitcoin.

There are plenty of scenarios, black swan and otherwise where Bitcoins can become a dominant force in the financial industry. There are plenty of doom and gloom scenarios you can think of where Bitcoin will retain it's worth and value as hyperinflation consumes the fiat currency of a weak central government (there has been at least one recorded case in Argentina where a person sold his house for Bitcoin). However, that's being too pessimistic. Even without anything bad happening, Bitcoin can happily live alongside the traditional currencies of the world.

Some of the greatest advantages of Bitcoin are realized in efficient markets. It can be broken down into a hundred million parts, each called a satoshi, as opposed to fiat that usually can be broken down only into a hundred parts. Also, transactions over this network are essentially free or sometimes need a small transaction fee to induce the miners. By small, we are talking about less than a tenth of a percent. Compare this to the 2-4% fee charged normally by the credit card companies and you being to see why this concept is so attractive.

So now that you're convinced that Bitcoin is here to stay for the long run, how to make use of this? It is still in very early stages of development and there are plenty of places where you can make some Bitcoin. Faucets, for example, are supported solely by advertising and captchas and don't have any catch - you enter your wallet id and you get free Bitcoins.

There are several other concepts from the Get-Paid-To world translated and made especially for the Bitcoin economy. For example, there are several ways in which you can take surveys, watch videos, and visit advertiser websites, all in exchange for some Bitcoins. This being new, it is a great way to test out the waters and secure some of these in the process. Remember that it is far easier to give away Bitcoins because micro-transactions are so convenient. There doesn't have to be a real minimum payout and even when there is, it is usually very minimal.

In order to participate in the Bitcoin economy, you don't need to be a technical expert or even delve very deep into the workings of the currency. There are several services you can use to make the process as simple as possible. In this book we mentioned the Blockchain and Coinbase Apps and websites, were you can exchange your Euros or US Dollars for Cryptocurrenices like Bitcoin. It is all up to you to take that leap of faith and stay in the game for the long run.

THANK YOU

Thank you again for purchasing this book!

I hope this book was able to help you understand how Bitcoins works, what the risks are and how to select the right platform to get your first Bitcoins for free or by buying them.

If you want to learn more about crypto currencies I advise you to visit the blog:

www.aboutcryptocurrencies.net

Here you will find free material and free videos about crypto currencies, how to setup your Wallets. You will as find some advanced online trainings.

Thank you and good luck!

BITCOIN
BTC AND BCH

WHAT IS THE DIFFERENCE?

BY

JOHAN VON AMSTERDAM

INTRODUCTION

Recently, the world of cryptocurrency has been awakened with the arrival and incredible growth of Bitcoin (BTC). Now the most successful cryptocurrency in history, BTC is on the rise, demanding the attention of savvy investors around the globe.

And with the growing attention comes, of course, growing controversy.

Much like a Kafka novel, the plot of Bitcoin is becoming more interesting with each day. As of August 1st, 2017, Bitcoin split into two factions: Bitcoin (BTC) and Bitcoin Cash (BCH). Wanting to become two distinct currencies, many investors are left wondering which side to choose and, more importantly, what exactly is the difference between the two.

As the story continues to be written, definite answers to some of our most exciting questions will be answered.

In the meantime, we need to make sure we are making the smartest decisions possible with our money, taking in to account both long and short term implications of BTC and BCH.

An essential guide for any cryptocurrency investor, we will address the major questions about this split and then look to the future for answers about what's next. A simple walk through a complicated minefield, you will discover Bitcoin's exciting history, the hidden features, and the most important underlying principles of this type of investing.

Feel confident in your investments and opinions - it's time to unlock the mystery behind Bitcoin's major split.

CHAPTER 1

INTRODUCTION TO CRYPTOCURRENCIES

WHAT IS CRYPTOCURRENCY

A cryptocurrency can be defined as a part of alternative currencies, virtual cash or digital asset that is intended for use as a medium of exchange while employing the use of cryptography as a technique to secure transactions and to take the creation of other units of the currency under management and control. For the sake of clarity, cryptography is the study of methods of creating and evaluating protocols that put a stop to third parties from reading concealed messages.

THE HISTORY OF CRYPTOCURRENCIES

The forerunners of today's cryptocurrencies are the "b-money," which was a proposal and concept in the late 90s on a digital monetary system published by Wei Dai, a computer Engineer, and the "Bit Gold," a precursor of Bitcoin that was created by Nick Szabo. In fact, Wei Dai's work and ideas were almost ~~much~~ identical to the Bitcoin scheme in use today, but he insisted that the concepts were developed independently of one another.

In 2009, a mysterious developer that goes by the pseudonym Satoshi Nakamoto created the first decentralized cryptocurrency, which is the bitcoin. Consequently, other cryptocurrencies such as Litecoin, Peercoinwas, Namecoin, Zcash, Dash, Ethereum, Rippx among several others have since come on board. Each of them has a broad range of features that seek to address specific issues plaguing the world of cryptocurrency.

FEATURES

- Owing to the technology and security attributes they possess, it is hard to make counterfeits of cryptocurrencies.

- Another essential characteristic of cryptocurrencies that might make them more appealing is the fact that they are organic; in essence it means that they are not created by a government or Central authority.

- What being decentralized means in effect is that they are, in theory, free from any form of meddling or manipulation.

- Unlike centralized currencies, nearly all cryptocurrencies are supposed to reduce in production in due course. For instance, Bitcoin is never going to exceed a market cap of 21 million coins that will be in circulation over time. *How do we know this?*

- Although a variety of cryptocurrency specifications are obtainable today, nearly all of them are the result of any of two protocols referred to as proof-of-work or proof-of stake.

- Every cryptocurrency often relies on a community of miners that help validate and process transactions with the use of their ASIC machines. Without a doubt, the contributions of miners are immense and invaluable in the sustenance of the entire system.

- Due to the cryptographic technology behind it, the users of cryptocurrencies are afforded some degree of anonymity making it hard for law enforcement agencies to seize them, unlike centralized currencies.

attaching wages, etc.
seizing bank accounts
paying taxes?

THE DOLLAR IS A CENTRALIZED CURRENCY

THE PROS AND CONS OF CRYPTOCURRENCIES

- Cryptocurrencies ensure the secure transfer of funds is carried out with ease.

- When compared with the amount charged by traditional financial institutions for the transfer of funds, the transmission of funds via cryptocurrencies comes at negligible processing fee, which makes it even more appealing to users.

- The technology behind the Bitcoin's blockchain which is a sort of online ledger that helps maintain every transaction that's ever been carried out by means of Bitcoins is being explored by experts for its potentials in crowdfunding, online voting and efficient processing of payments that could bring about a reduction of transaction fees in the Banking industry.

- Due to the inherent nature of cryptocurrencies as virtual or digital money which is lacking a centralized repository, their balances are more susceptible to complete obliteration during a system crash, especially if no backup is maintained. Furthermore, their online ledgers may be prone to attacks from hackers.

- The market prices of cryptocurrencies are dependent on sentiments that fuels supply and demand, thereby making the rate at which they are exchanged move backward and forward widely.

CHAPTER 2

THE BASICS OF BITCOIN

As stated earlier, Bitcoin is a digital currency that was created in 2009 by Satoshi Nakamoto who mined the first Bitcoin circulation. Bitcoin is one of the pioneering cryptocurrencies that employ the use of a peer-to-peer payment technology to aid in facilitating immediate payments or transactions. Being a virtual currency like all cryptocurrencies, Bitcoin is not owned by banks, stock exchanges, organization, governments, and company.

THE WORKINGS OF BITCOIN

BITCOIN ESSENTIALS

- For new users to get familiarized with the use of Bitcoin, they must first obtain Bitcoin wallet software that will help encrypt and maintain Bitcoin balances on either their computer or mobile phone devices.

- Since most wallet software is downloadable, all you have to do is to download and install it on your device.

- As soon as you have installed wallet software on any device of your choice, you may generate a Bitcoin address and share it with people to make a payment to you or for you to pay to them. You can generate as many Bitcoin addresses as your need for safety. A Bitcoin address must only be utilized on one occasion for your anonymity to be sustained.

- The investor can purchase Bitcoins via other payment means like credit card or bank account and fill up their wallet with the Bitcoins

- The adoption of Bitcoin as a medium of exchange is fast gaining popularity as it can be employed to settle transactions at dentists, groceries, clothing stores, online retailers, vehicle purchases, restaurants, and even for property rentals.

- Aside from using it to make payments for purchases, you can also make a fortune from speculating in Bitcoin itself. Such speculation centers on staking Bitcoins in the hope that it will go up in value.

- The least unit of Bitcoin is the Satoshi and is gotten when Bitcoin is divided into eight decimal places, which is 100 millionth of one Bitcoin. If the majority miners agree to the change, Bitcoin could still be further split into more decimal places.

This is how inflation happens?

67

UNDERSTANDING THE BLOCKCHAIN

A blockchain is the shared public ledger upon which the whole Bitcoin network is dependent. It is a record of all transactions that's ever been carried out. The blockchain is regularly on the increase and being updated with fresh records of "blocks" that are deemed to have been 'completed.' To understand this above explanation clearly, you may consider it as a way of assessing the spendable balance of a Bitcoin wallet and to verify new transactions to be Bitcoins that can be spent and are really owned by the individual spending them.

FEATURES OF THE BLOCKCHAIN

- The introduction of blocks to the blockchain is done in a linear, chronological order.

- Cryptography is used to ensure the security, integrity and chronological order of the blockchain system.

- Every computer (node) that is linked to the Bitcoin network with the intention of carrying out the validation and conveyance of transactions can automatically access a downloadable copy of the blockchain upon being linked with the Bitcoin network.

- It maintains full information concerning the addresses and their balances right from the origin of the block to the recently completed block.

HOW DOES BLOCKCHAIN WORK?

The block itself is a 'current' aspect of a blockchain that accounts for some or all of the latest transactions, and as soon as it is complete, it moves straight to the blockchain as a long-lasting part of the database. The blockchain is a register of all the transactions on the Bitcoin network. The blockchain is viewed as a significant technological advancement.

Every time a block becomes complete, a new one is created, and the blockchain has a limitless number of similar blocks in its system. You might want to think that the blocks are not well arranged or arbitrarily positioned in a blockchain, but, in reality, they are connected in an appropriate linear, chronological order, much in the same way chains are linked to one another, with each block holding a hash of the preceding block.

When drawing the comparison of the Bitcoin blockchain system with the traditional banking methods, blockchain can be linked to an entire history of records of banking transactions. Another area of similarity is that transactions are chronologically inputted in a blockchain much in the same way bank transactions are entered. Furthermore, blocks can be compared to bank statements.

Every computer or node that takes part in the operation of the system can have access to the blockchain database and is dependent on the Bitcoin protocol in use. The complete copy of the blockchain contains detailed account and history of all Bitcoin transactions ever performed.

It can thus provide insight as regards detailed information on a specific Bitcoin address; such as how much worth or value can be attributed to it at any point in its history. The growing popularity of Bitcoin as a cryptocurrency has resulted in an enormous increase in transactions, and it is estimated that a new block is added to the blockchain via mining at an average about 10 minutes apiece. It is important to note that the ever-rising size of the blockchain is regarded by some stakeholders as problematic due to lack of storage and time to harmonize.

WHAT ARE BITCOIN BLOCKS?

Blocks can be defined as files in which data relating to the Bitcoin network is entered or recorded in a lasting manner. The block is designed in such a way that it takes account of several or every one of the most recent Bitcoin transactions that haven't been captured in any past blocks.

As a result, the block functions in the same way as a page of a bank ledger or record book. As soon as a block is deemed to be 'completed,' it gives up to the subsequent block in the blockchain. Another key feature of a block is that it maintains a lasting store of records, which as soon as it is written, can't be changed or gotten rid of.

In summary, since the Bitcoin network is subject to a significant amount of transactional activities, it becomes pertinent to keep an evidence of these transactions so that users can follow the trail of what's been paid, to whom and by whom. The block directly takes a record of transactions that's been carried out within a particular period.

CHAPTER 3

BITCOIN PROTOCOLS

The inherent and underlying issues that are often associated with the traditional cryptocurrency ~~made~~ caused Bitcoin to come up with the use of the blockchain protocol to manage the entire system because Bitcoin is one of the first peer-to-peer payment networks that also works based on a cryptographic protocol. In reality, no particular individual can lay claim to ownership of the bitcoin protocol, but we shall examine the workings of the protocol and also take a look at the major Bitcoin protocols.

HOW DOES BITCOIN PROTOCOL WORK?

Owners of Bitcoins can send and receive coins by just broadcasting digitally signed messages to the network via their bitcoin wallet's software. Since the existing Bitcoin transaction system is reliant on trust, users can only hope that each transaction will bring about a specific outcome. However, the issue is that these electronic payment systems are not to be relied on infrequently, thereby resulting in apprehension about fraud between buyers and sellers.

The problem of deceit or unreliability might be the result of a variety of factors that range from users trying to double-spend their coins or a user making an effort to refuse service from another user or a user looking for ways to exploit the system for financial gains. As a way of putting a check on the issues as mentioned earlier and other possible attacks that may arise; Bitcoin developers set up a system that is dependent on cryptographic proof via the utilization of digital signatures and a very complicated verification process.

USING DIGITAL SIGNATURES FOR VERIFICATION

Blockchain employs the use of a series of digital signatures known as "coin," that is received as soon as a holder passes it on to the next owner. Every time it is transferred, the owner inserts a hash that indicates the past transactions and the public key of the new holder. As the electronic coin goes from one owner to another, notations are all included at the end of it, so as to give a way to verify ownership.

Coin is a digital signature

EXTRA LAYER OF TRUST USING TIMESTAMP SERVER AND PROOF-OF-WORK SYSTEM

As a way of ensuring that the same value of coins are not spent more than once or "double spent," Bitcoin developers set up a verification process that determines how the coin is being used. The process employs the use of a timestamp server that inserts a period in time to the hash to confirm or verify the transaction. In addition to that, the timestamp is integrated, together with each change in possession of the coin. Furthermore, a proof-of-work system applies a specific value to the electronic coin to further authenticate every transaction that is carried out with the cryptocurrency.

THE BLOCKCHAIN NETWORK

As mentioned earlier, Bitcoin as a cryptocurrency is decentralized in the sense that it employs a network format whereby fresh transactions are stored into blocks. Afterward, the value or a proof-of-work is added to the block and then relayed throughout the network. Acceptance of the blocks of digital coins is only possible after they have been confirmed and verified as being spent.

New blocks will continue to go through the process of sustaining the movement of the digital coins from one owner to another and being tracked whether it has been spent on specific goods or services with the blockchain network which is also regarded as a kind of ledger. As soon as sufficient blocks are generated from the digital coins, they can then be gotten rid of, to make more disk space available to hold newer blocks.

LINKING CHAINS

MAINTAINING AN HONEST LEDGER

Due to the common threat of fraud that the conventional transaction system was well-known for, it becomes essential for blockchain to try to find a way to make sure that those dealing with these blocks are as sincere as possible. What it means, in essence, is that, for those to whom the task of verifying and recording transactions (miners) on the block to remain honest and sincere, they are to be compensated by way of their digital coins as recompense for honest work.

This way, miners become conscious of the fact that, adhering to the regulations of blockchain is more ~~a great deal is~~ beneficial than trying to ~~to try and~~ con the system. Miners are individuals or organizations with machines that verify a transaction and add ~~include~~ it to the public blockchain so that other miners can have the right to use and bring up to date their own version of the blockchain. For their role and the work they carry out on the blockchain network, miners get rewarded with a little portion of each transaction they execute.

On the other hand, there are a number of backup procedures, which are often in operation on the network or business-owned machines that Bitcoin developers have adopted and enforced to thwart any attack or to prevent bad blocks from the network. A typical case in point of a backup course of action is network alerts which may have been fashioned to go off, once miners discover these bad blocks. Afterward, the alerts and doubtful blocks are pulled and evaluated for any contradictions and then taken out if they are discovered to be invalid.

HOW BLOCKCHAIN FOSTERS PRIVACY AND ANONYMITY

Bitcoin is able to guarantee the privacy of users because the blockchain technology only gives an idea that an individual is sending something to someone else without giving a clue about what is being sent and whether it has to do with currency, information, or any other form of valuable asset. The elimination of a dependable third party and counterparty attaches a degree of privacy to the use of electronic cash for transactions. In this fashion, the process of employing the use of cryptocurrency such as Bitcoin gives the holder some degree of anonymity.

MAJOR BITCOIN PROTOCOLS

The growth of Bitcoin as a cyptocurrency since its origin in 2009 has been on a meteoric rise both in size and scope with its notional value reaching in excess of $10 billion and so has its network grown at an exponential rate as well. All through this development, the system started to go through various pains linked to such growth, and they are widely related to scaling up, in order to create room for the huge number and rate of transactions, while maintaining the security, intrinsic value ~~worth~~ of privacy, and reduced transaction costs all at once.

At this stage, it is crucial to bear in mind that the novel protocol that was written by Bitcoin's founder, the mysterious Satoshi Nakamoto has turned out to be known as Bitcoin core or Bitcoin QT. And it has led to three rival versions of the Bitcoin protocol; which are the BitPay Core, Bitcoin Classic and Bitcoin Unlimited. The three attempts came in the wake of a contentious roll out of Bitcoin XT that might have resulted in an increase of the block size to 8MB but were mostly rejected by the bitcoin community.

BITPAY CORE

Although BitPay Core is in a trial phase for now, however, its fundamental concept revolves around having two limits. Number one is a 'hard limit' on block size that would be altered on a frequent basis, coinciding with intricate adjustments, and a second 'soft limit' which the miner community will want to make compulsory among themselves and is comparable to the focal points of Bitcoin Unlimited.

BITCOIN CLASSIC

This Bitcoin protocol aims to take the edge off the issues of huge transactions that are leading to transaction log jams and rising transaction costs. The protocol hoped to achieve this by way of increasing the block size, which is the quantity of kilobyte in a block of transactions from 1MB to 2MB. The choice of 2MB was selected on purpose and was dependent on the results of data gathered by its developers, and from interactions with several Bitcoin miners and mining pools. Aside from the support, it has from big mining pools like AntPooland BW Pool, and wallet/exchanges such as Coinbase and OKCoin, the creators of Bitcoin classic states that they have the backing of Gavin Andresen, the past Bitcoin Core lead and Bitcoin XT developer.

BITCOIN UNLIMITED

This Bitcoin protocol as the name implies embraces the nonexistence of a hard-coded block-size limit. As a substitute, it lets users set limits on their nodes manually; the developers look ahead to a compromise on a limit to materialize naturally at an ostensibly Schelling or focal point. The protocol is designed to be a solution that people will be inclined to exploit in the absence of communication since it appears natural, unique, or valuable to them. In addition, it aims to bring in some degree of democracy by letting the community to vote on necessary changes regarding how to develop, manage and implement the protocol.

CHAPTER 4

BITCOIN PRIVATE KEYS

A Bitcoin private key can be described as a secret number created to let people spend their Bitcoins or make irreversible transactions. Users are given a Bitcoin private key when they are issued with a Bitcoin address. Typically, it has a 256-bit number and may be used to sell, accept, donate Bitcoin, hence must be kept really safe. For instance, a Bitcoin private key may look like this: 18Qs4IuA5d5ViEiPWYau6fhRTHEFZ9XaLo.

KEEPING YOUR PRIVATE KEYS SAFE

In the past, several secret/private keys or backup seed have been lost due to the storage medium on which they are saved. Frequently used mediums of storing private keys are listed below with some of their weaknesses.

STORAGE ON A PIECE OF PAPER

Whether the information is written, printed or laminated, a number of things could go wrong with the storage medium, and they are not limited to the following:

- The paper may be discovered and stolen

- The paper could be torn, burnt, spoiled, or damaged by smoke

- A hand-written paper might not be legible; laminated paper is susceptible to being ruined while attempts to print on paper could be unsuccessful if the paper is wet.

STORAGE ON A FLASH DRIVE

- The possibility of breakage exists

- It can be affected by fast changing magnetic fields, for example, MRIs

- They may be affected by fire and smoke

- Many of these drives are not designed for storing things in the long run

- Can become corroded from salt water or some atmospheric conditions

- You may find it hard to retrieve your data from it

- It can be adversely affected by harsh environmental factors

- In general, flash drives aren't recommended for long-term storage

STORAGE IN THE CLOUD

- There is a risk of hackers attempting to steal the private keys

- Other people may have access to your cloud storage and take the keys

STORAGE ON A COMPUTER

- They are susceptible to crashes which make data recovery costly

- Computers are prone to physical attacks and may get burnt or damaged by smoke

- The data on conventional hard disc drive may be degraded by strong magnetic fields and could get destroyed physically.

- Mishaps might occur that will bring about data loss

- It is ill-advised to store up data meant to last for long on Solid state drives (SSDs) if they are not going to be powered.

- If the computer is linked to the internet, it is prone to attacks from hackers who might want to break into it, to steal the key irrespective of the encryption technology employed.

- The use of a computer for storage of private keys is often associated with a broad range of threats like firmware exploits, the use of malicious USB cords and 0-day exploits.

- The use external hard disk drives for storage are limited to just couple of years as a minimum if stored appropriately

- If computer is not linked to the net, the safety it provides is function of the encryption technology used and doesn't negate the fact that an individual may still enter the location illegally and copy the data with no one taking notice

STORAGE ON DIGITAL MEDIA LIKE CD, FLOPPY DISK, LASERDISC, OR MINI-DISC

- There is a high tendency for plastics to stop working after a while.

- Exposure to adverse environmental conditions such as heat, humidity, regular light, all kind of chemicals, and the oxygen in the air may degrade them. It could also result in data loss when private keys are stored on a medium derived from plastic or written/printed on plastic.

- Plastics could get burnt or become damaged by smoke

- The risk of bodily harm occurring exist, thereby making it not viable or costly to recover the lost data

- There is a probability that magnetic media such as tapes and floppy disc could be damaged by magnetic fields

CHAPTER 5

BETWEEN A HARD
AND A SOFT FORK!

Bitcoin is based on open source software, which implies that the code is free and accessible for everyone to view and make use of. For individuals or organizations contributing in the Bitcoin network whether as miners, node operators, or wallet administrators; staying up-to-date regarding the versions of the Bitcoin software code is essential.

With the evolution of Bitcoin as a cryptocurrency, it becomes imperative that several adjustments have to be made to the protocol. These alterations may range from including new feature sets like allowing multi-sig, to altering a core metric of the protocol, such as raising the peak block size.

THE ELEPHANT IN THE ROOM

The core issue is with the speed of the technology which is really slow. Bitcoin network processes around seven transactions in 10 minutes compared to VISA that handles 150 million transactions every day. VISA deals with 1700 transactions per second, and its system has the ability to handle 24000 each second. Users of Bitcoin are increasing every day, and there's no alteration to the core technology that handles their transactions, thereby resulting in network logjams and extensive waiting period for transactions to go through.

THE RUDIMENTS OF FORKS

It is important to note that before now, Bitcoin forks takes place somewhat on a regular basis. A fork is the side-effect of distributed consensus that occurs whenever two miners locate a block almost at the same time. To put it simply, a fork in software development alludes to an event that results in an independent project spinning off from a software project.

The resolution of the uncertainty around such events becomes apparent when successive blocks are added to one, thereby causing it to become the lengthiest chain, whereas the other block becomes "orphaned" or neglected by the network.

However, forks could as well be deliberately set up in the network, and often comes about when developers try to make amends to the rules that the software utilizes to make a decision on whether a transaction is valid or not. For instance, Litecoin, a cryptocurrency is a fork of Bitcoin since the creators of Litecoin copied Bitcoin's code, carried out some alterations, and then launched a separate project.

As soon as a block is found to have transactions that are invalid, then it is disregarded by the network, and the miner who discovers that block will miss out on a block recompense. Consequently, miners, in general, would like to mine only blocks that are valid and built on the longest chain. It is vital to keep in mind that changes induced to a protocol often call for either a soft or hard fork of the Bitcoin software. Performing a fork of the Bitcoin software is different from other open source projects since each user operating a Bitcoin node have to sustain their compatibility with the network.

The implication is that any miner that is making use of a Bitcoin software version that isn't suited to the version all and sundry are using may find themselves mining the wrong Blockchain. Nevertheless, miners may bring different versions of the Bitcoin software into play and mine the same Blockchain if the varying versions are well-matched. Here, compatibility is very vital.

Below are some the more widely known forks and their characteristics:

HARD FORK

A hard fork can be described as a software upgrade that sets up a new rule to the network which isn't well-matched with the older software. It could be merely regarded as an extension of the rules. For example, a new rule that permits block size to be 2MB in place of 1MB would have need of a hard fork. A hard fork is complicated in nature as it is an alteration of the Bitcoin protocol, which isn't backward compatible with older versions of the client.

When a hard fork takes place, Nodes that keep on operating on the old version of the software will find newer transactions on the network as being invalid. However, for the entire community to carry on mining valid blocks, every single one of the nodes in the network would have to upgrade to the new rules.

WHAT ARE THE RISKS?

When a hard fork occurs, it could lead to a lot of issues that are not limited to the political fallout that may take place when some sort of political impasse arises, and a fraction of the community prefers to stand by the old rules come what may. In this case, the network computing power or hash rate behind the old chain makes no difference. In fact, what counts the most is the data rule set, since the data is still supposed to have value, which means miners are keen to mine a chain and developers are apt to prop it up. A typical case of how a community might be torn apart over rules is the Ethereum DAO hard fork that resulted in two blockchains employing a variation of the software (Ethereum and Ethereum classic) with both having dissimilar philosophy and currencies.

When a hard fork is performed, the principal risk that may occur is a circumstance whereby nodes on the network using the new software are separated from the earlier version, leading to a fork of the Blockchain. For instance, you may find half of the nodes on the network are using the latest version and mining blocks while the remaining half are mining a different set of blocks by running the older version of the software; which in essence means you will get two dissimilar chains giving rise to a fork of the Blockchain. The scenario given above is quite different from a software fork.

SOFT FORK

On the other hand, a soft fork is any alteration that is backward compatible. For example, a new rule could just let 500 Kilobyte blocks as an alternative to 1MB block. In this situation, nodes that have not been upgraded to be compatible with the new rule will see the new transactions as valid because 500 kilobyte is below 1MB in this scenario. But, should the nodes that haven't been upgraded to be compatible with the new rules keep on mining blocks, the blocks they mine won't be recognized by the nodes that have been updated and rejected as a result. It is for this reason that soft forks require a greater part hash power in the network.

WHAT ARE THE RISKS?

A soft fork that doesn't get a majority of hash power in the network implies that it has very little support and may turn out to be the shortest chain and thus, become orphaned by the network. Otherwise, it may behave in the same vein as a hard fork whereby one chain might just break off. But, if members of the community find it hard to reach a consensus and are separated by such an issue, then the old and new version of Bitcoin might emerge as distinct projects from then on.

It is not all gloom with soft forks because they have mainly been the frequently used choice to upgrade the Bitcoin blockchain nearly all the time, as it is believed that they offer a lesser risk of tearing the network apart. In the past, some soft forks that have gone quite well consists of the P2SH that resulted in the alteration of Bitcoin's address formatting, and the BIP 66 that took care of Bitcoin's signature validation.

USER-ACTIVATED SOFT FORK (UASF)

A user-activated soft fork (UASF) can be described as a contentious proposal that looks at the way a blockchain could add an upgrade, which isn't backed, directly by those stakeholders who makes the network's hashing or computing power available.

The concept of UASF aims to work on the basis that rather than wait for a threshold of support from mining pools, the authority to trigger a soft fork should go to the exchanges, wallets, and companies who are using full nodes. A full node is seen in Bitcoin as one that is still in charge of validating blocks, even though it may not be a mining node.

A greater fraction of key exchanges may have to publicly give their backing to the change, ahead of it being written into a new version of the code. Subsequently, the new software that has been assigned a starting point in the future becomes installed on nodes that would like to partake in the soft fork.

WHAT ARE THE RISKS?

This approach calls for a much longer lead time for it to work than a soft fork that is hash-power-triggered. In fact, it is assumed it could take as much as a year or more to write the code and get all and sundry geared up.

Additionally, if nearly all of the miners end up not agreeing to activate the new rules, they may bring into play their remarkable hash power to divide the network. At present this proposal is hypothetical and hasn't been put into operation.

CHAPTER 6

BTC VERSUS BCH

Bitcoin (BTC) is the popular cryptocurrency that's known all over the world for many years, while in contrast, Bitcoin Cash (BCH) is the projected hard fork that maintained it is closest to Satoshi Nakamoto's original idea for the currency. In order words, BTC and BCH are probable forks of the Bitcoin blockchain.

Before August 1st, 2017 there was a huge debate over the validity of BCH because there was uncertainty whether mining organizations would begin to assign hashing power to it. A move that could end up making it a valid, usable currency with enhanced scalability than the real Bitcoin (BTC) itself, and might even surpass the price of Bitcoin swiftly and turn out to be the default online currency. Otherwise, it might end up being worthless or just like any alt coin out there.

The root of the problem pertains to Bitcoin's legacy code and its capacity of 1MB of data for each block, or around three transactions for every second. The debate had raged for over a year concerning a 'consensus' solution to the problem. Some few days earlier, most key members of, the community had agreed to an upgrade known as Segwit(Segregated Witness) that was locked-in to be wholly put into operation by November 2017.

However, BCH was at variance with the philosophy of Segwit and then made known its plan to increase the block size limit to 8MB by setting off the User Activated Hard Fork (UAHF) on August 1, 2017. Again, supporters of Bitcoin cash considered SegWit to be going against some essential strong points of Bitcoin, such as its decentralization and democratization.

Additionally, they also think SegWit2x was being led by persons with links to shady organizations, and that SegWit2x could be the end of Bitcoin as it is known.

END OF THE ROAD FOR BITCOIN BEFORE IT FORKS

BCH

With its proposal, Bitcoin Cash (BCH) plans to resolve these problems, and it is crucial to bear in mind that one of the most remarkable things about Bitcoin Cash (BCH) is that it gives room for custom block sizing. The increased block size of 8MB proposed by BCH is expected to speed up verification process, and ultimately ensure the survival of the network in spite of the number of miners backing it, albeit with some adjustable degree of difficulty. Its key features include:

- Bitcoin Cash is lead by a client that is referred to as BitcoinABC; where the ABC means "Adjustable Blocksize Cap." In essence, it implies that users may determine their favored blocksize as a result.

- The BCH's default blocksize is set to 2MB, and it has the potential for users to scale it up to 16MB.

- On its official website, BCH defines its currency as being the same as Satoshi's original vision for the coin. It goes on to affirm that "Bitcoin Cash is peer-to-peer electronic cash for the Internet. It is entirely decentralized, with no central bank and requires no trusted third parties to operate."

SEGWIT2X

As the August 1st deadline drew nearer, one of two key proposals for enhancing bitcoin's transactional capacity is the SEGWIT2X, which may have gained the most interest. It has the support of a considerable number of prestigious Bitcoin organizations and individuals, the majority of whom are directly associated with the system's startup and investment community. They include nearly all the network's big mining pools, prominent developers such as Gavin Andresen of Bitcoin Core, Bitcoin startups such as Blockchain, BitPay, and Coinbase, among several others.

FEATURES

- SEGWIT was an optimization put forward by Bitcoin Core developer Pieter Wuille in 2015 that aims to increase the number of transactions that go into every block with no need to raise the block size parameter. In particular, it also takes away the problem of transaction malleability, which may result in a significant improvement of the network if resolved.

- The alterations proposed by SEGWIT2X seek to update the software rules to give room for 2MB blocks. Other rivals with similar objectives to raise Bitcoin's block size parameter such as Bitcoin Unlimited, Bitcoin XT and Bitcoin Classic do not have the same level support as SEGWIT2X.

- Before August 1st, 2017, SEGWIT2X wasn't suggested nor sanctioned by Bitcoin Core, the network's major open-source developer team.

- SEGWIT2X will perform long-anticipated code optimization Segregated Witness (SegWit) that changes the way some data is amassed on the network.

- Its ideas and proposals aren't as fresh but only bring together those proposed earlier by other developers in a new manner.

- As soon as SegWit is activated, it sets a timeline of three months (November 2017), to raise the network's block size from 1MB all the way up to 2MB.

UPDATE

The primary aspect of SegWit2x known as BIP91 was locked-in and triggered some days before the scheduled August 1, while BIP148 was to be set off on that day itself. Having locked-in BIP91, a lot of people believed the likelihood of a hard fork was over, but supporters of BCH seem to have other ideas.

CHAPTER 7

THE SPLIT!

A TALE OF TWO BITCOIN

On the morning of August 1st, 2017, an attempt to generate another version of the bitcoin blockchain was formally making progress. After overcoming some obstacles that morning, miners managed to create a block on a new blockchain successfully, called Bitcoin Cash at 18:24:41 UTC.

- Then, ViaBTC pool created a 1.9 MB BCH block that wasn't valid on the legacy Bitcoin network. This move, in fact, marked a break away from the major bitcoin network and taking the lead with a different technical plan.

- In general, the event occurred almost six hours after block 478,558 – the point at which miners made efforts to begin the split.

- Data from the network reveals that the BCH block had 6,985 transactions, with a block size of 1.915 MB which was almost two times the size of this parameter on the original chain. The data point is noteworthy since BCH was intended to boost network capacity by providing a blockchain with a bigger block size.

THE BITCOIN SPLIT

SUPPORT FROM BITCOIN PROVIDERS

As long as your Bitcoins are securely held in a personal wallet, the likelihood of losing your cashcoins is very slim. But, there is a slim chance that malicious miners could attempt to pilfer your coins when you attempt to make Bitcoin transactions. In trying to prevent this risk from occurring you may have to divide the coins into different Bitcoin and Bitcoin Cash wallets. Some wallets have given specific updates, services, and instructions for splitting coins.

Ahead of the August 1st, 2017 events, some major exchanges, and wallet providers gave their strategy for the hard fork. Many stated that they wouldn't back BCH at all; some said they would support it as an altcoin that will let users split their coins if they want.

But none of the businesses affirmed that they would back BCH as the number one, genuine Bitcoin. As an alternative, they declared an intention to support Bitcoin itself, or endorse the longest chain, which means that they would support any of the blockchain that emerged triumphantly.

Below are a list of leading Bitcoin exchanges and their position on sustaining BCH trading.

- Coinbase: will reject BCH

- BitMEX: will reject BCH

- Bitstamp: will reject BCH

- Bittrex: agreed

- Kraken: agreed

- OkCoin: agreed

- Poloniex: Possibly

- BTCC: agreed

- Gemini: will wait to see if BCH is viable

- Fitbit: will reject BCH

- ViaBTC: Yes, at a 1:1 ratio

Important note:

The most of above Bitcoin exchanges, which initially rejected Bitcoin cash trading, are altered their vision after lawsuits and pressure from the Bitcoin user community and decided the support the trade of Bitcoin cash in the (near) future.

From its website, wallets that support Bitcoin cash (BCH) ahead of the 1st of August event include the following:

- BitcoinUnlimited

- BitcoinABC

- Ledger

- ElectrumCash

- FreeWallet

- BitcoinClassic

- BXT

- Trezor

- BTC.com

- AirBitz

- Coinomi

Some major wallets have the following opinion about BCH:

Blockchain.info

It is crucial that owners of Blockchain wallets retain their wallet and associated recovery phrase and not delete them, even though they may empty the BTC balance. It supports withdrawals from exchanges that won't support BCH.

Electrum

Despite the fact that the most recent version of Electrum, 2.9, is able to make a distinction between rival chains, Electrum doesn't back Bitcoin Cash formally. In reality, Electrum believes the "Electrum Cash" fork of their software to be a trademark violation.

Ledger

Ledger is a trendy hardware wallet that supports Bitcoin Cash. Also, its wallet interface will feature a split utility and a selector for the two chains.

Exodus

Exodus doubles as a wallet and exchange service outlet, and doesn't provide support for BCH, either via splitting or providing a market.

Jaxx

Users on this platform are usually in charge of their private keys, and matching Bitcoin Cash (BCH) ought to be secure in your Jaxx wallet. But, users have to bear in mind that they won't be able to access/send/receive their Bitcoin Cash (BCH) pending when the integration occurs.

CHAPTER 8

AFTERMATH OF THE
BITCOIN SPLIT

BTC AND BCH

Some days after Bitcoin (BTC) had gone through an upgrade
and a currency split, the foremost Cryptocurrency looks as if
it has outlived one of the most tumultuous periods in its
lifetime. The question you'd want to ask is, how has Bitcoin
fared after this controversial and massive split? The outcome
has thus far been splendid for Bitcoin. Everything appears to
be getting back to normal, as confidence in the currency
continues to soar with miners, traders, exchanges, and users
of Bitcoin all going about their business as usual.

On the day that the split took place, the price of BTC which
had been on a recovery to its former level a few days before
August 1st, 2017, fell in value from $2,875 to $2718,
representing about 5% drop. On the other hand, Bitcoin Cash
(BCH) surpassed Ripple to turn out to be the third largest
cryptocurrency, by trading at around $400 levels. Some few
hours later BCH's price movement became livelier and was
trading in the region of $700 and having a market

capitalization that went past $11 billion, representing nearly11% of the general market capitalization.

THE IMPACT OF THE SPLIT ON`ETHERIUM

Some days before the split, Bitcoin (BTC) dropped about 10% to below $2,500 level in value owing to uncertainty over the impending upgrade and split. But it on the 1st of August, Ethereum (ETH) experienced a rise that pushed it tidily clear of $220 levels.

WHAT DOES THE FUTURE HOLD FOR BTC AND BCH

As at the time of writing this ebook, Bitcoin (BTC) just flew past the $3,500 level, which indicates a high degree of confidence in the number one cryptocurrency. With the second phase of the implementation of its upgrade still looming ahead on 1st of November 2017, which is a hard fork that is not backward compatible with older Bitcoin clients and will double the Bitcoin's block size to 2MB. When the result is coupled with the increase in block size limit that SEGWIT will bring about, then Bitcoin (BTC) should have a total maximum of 8MB of block space.

If the upgrade goes according to plan, then Bitcoin should continue to soar. Expectedly, BTC ought to continue with its rise in value than other cryptocurrencies and keep on enjoying a majority of the market capitalization. Perhaps we might see it reaching the $5,000 before the end of the year. It should remain safe and secure to use, but it would be hard to tell how its processing speed will be like in future. Furthermore, if other stakeholders in the community feel some of the core principles of Bitcoin such as its decentralized nature and democratic potentials of the blockchain technology is being compromised, then they might move on to other cryptocurrencies that have exciting possibilities and appeals to them.

BTC POWER

As for BCH, it is currently trading at $340 but may likely rise in value in due time, if it is able to get miners to invest sufficient hash power to its network. Several estimates have it that BCH is able to attract 4% of miners to itself, making it vulnerable to attacks from malicious actors who manage some of these computing powers, and the only way they can prevent such attacks is to get close 50% of the Bitcoin's hash rate. That's why BCH's value might be just a fraction of BTC in the long run. However, if the SEGWIT changes make a lot of people unhappy, and they decide to switch over to BCH then its hash power might go up considerably.

Thank you!

Thank you again for purchasing this book!

I hope this book was able to help you to understand more regarding the technical language used in the world of Bitcoin and cryptocurrencies in general.

Keep up-to-date and learn more on my blog:

http://aboutcryptocurrencies.net

Here you will find free material and free videos about Bitcoin and cryptocurrencies. You can learn how to setup your Bitcoin Wallet. You will as find some advanced online trainings.

Finally, if you enjoyed this book, then I'd like to ask you for a favor, would you be kind enough to leave a review for this book on Amazon? It'd be greatly appreciated!

https://www.amazon.com/dp/B0752WTM1M/

Thank you for reading and I want to wish you the best in the world of cryptocurrencies!

public key
private key

QR code

iOS

Android

ether

litecoin

Coinbase

CPSIA information can be obtained
at www.ICGtesting.com
Printed in the USA
LVOW11s0320190218
567094LV00009B/235/P